ROMANS

PRINCETON ■ LONDON

What's in the book

4 **The Roman world**
The lands ruled by the Roman empire

6 **Roman towns**
Typical features of a Roman town

8 **The city of Rome**
As it was in Roman times and as it is today

10 **Republic and emperors**
The power of the people

12 **The Roman army**
Attention! Roman soldiers are ready for inspection

14 **Slaves**
Overworked and underpaid!

16 **Gods and temples**
Investigate the Romans' religious beliefs

18 **Roman characters**
A range of characters from Roman times

20 **Roman baths**
Enjoy a relaxing trip to the baths

22 **Farming**
Working the land in Roman times

*All words in the text that appear in **bold** can be found in the glossary*

24 **Food**
Feast your eyes on a Roman menu

26 **A Roman house**
Take a look inside a Roman house

28 **Clothes**
A guide to Roman style

29 **Romulus and Remus**
The legend of the two brothers

34 **How we know**
The evidence that's been left behind

35 **Glossary**
Key words defined

38 **Work book**
Note pages for you to photocopy and use

42 **Draw your own Roman city**
Create your own picture

44 **Questions and answers**
Answer all your questions about the Romans

46 **Index**
The quick route to reference checking

The Roman world

According to legend, the Roman civilization began in 753 BC. Between 300 BC and AD 200, the Romans conquered many countries and created a huge empire. At its peak, the Roman empire spanned almost 3,500 miles from Britain to Egypt, including all the lands surrounding the Mediterranean Sea. It survived until AD 450 and was one of the greatest empires in history.

The Romans built cities and roads throughout their empire. They also taught the people in the lands they conquered how to live like Romans – to wear Roman clothes, worship Roman gods, and speak **Latin**, the language that the Romans used.

The Romans firmly believed that their own way of life was the best. They thought they were doing other people a favor by showing them the proper way to live.

FastFact
The Roman empire reached its greatest extent from AD 116–117, under the leadership of Emperor Trajan.

● Byzantium (Istanbul)

MACEDONIA

ASIA MINOR

● Athenae (Athens)

GREECE

Euphrates

Tigris

SYRIA

Hierosolyma (Jerusalem) ●

Alexandria ● **EGYPT**

Nile

Goods from all over the empire were brought to Rome by ship. Olives came from Spain, for example, and corn was harvested in Egypt.

Roman towns

Throughout their mighty empire, the Romans built many towns and cities, each housing between 3,000 and 10,000 people. Most cities, despite being in different countries, were built to the same plan and were divided by straight streets into a regular grid-like pattern. The larger towns all had similar buildings within them.

▼ Temple
A large Roman town usually had many temples. Most were out of bounds to ordinary people. Temples were built in honor of a different god or goddess.

Roman cemetery ▶
Roman cemeteries were always built outside the walls of their towns to reduce the risk of disease spreading. Wealthy people could afford spectacular tombs made of marble with beautiful carvings. The bodies of the poor, however, were often just dumped in a pit.

Amphitheatre ▶
The amphitheater was a large stadium where games were played in front of huge crowds, up to 50,000 in number. The so-called games were actually violent and bloody displays of combat in which gladiators fought to the death. Gladiators usually fought each other with different weapons; occasionally they fought wild animals.

Aqueduct ▶
Aqueducts carried fresh water from lakes, rivers, and springs to the cities and towns. Rome itself had 11 aqueducts to provide its water supply. Some wealthy people had water piped directly to their houses. Everyone else collected water in buckets from a tap or fountain in the street.

▼ Bathhouse
Public baths were more than just a place to wash. People also exercised, played games, and met with friends. Some baths even had their own libraries for visitors to borrow scrolls to read. Bathers would often have three baths, one warm, one hot, and one cold.

FastFact
A huge network of roads connected each main province to Rome.

◀ Forum
The forum was a large square found in every Roman town, where farmers and local traders sold their goods on market days. There were also public toilets and a fountain where people could collect fresh water. The citizens of the town came to the forum to discuss the town's affairs and to hear speeches by their leaders.

◀ Domus
A **domus** was a large house that would have belonged to a wealthy citizen. Ordinary Romans lived in small over-crowded apartments. Houses this size had several bedrooms, a dining room, a kitchen, a living room, servants' quarters, and a garden. Fresh running water and toilets were connected to a sewer, and hot air circulating underneath the floor tiles warmed the house.

◀ Town walls
Town walls were built to protect the town from attack. On top of the wall was a walkway for the soldiers to patrol. The only way into the town was through the big, heavy gates of one of the gatehouses. The gatehouses usually had rooms for the soldiers, an armory for storing weapons, and cells for prisoners.

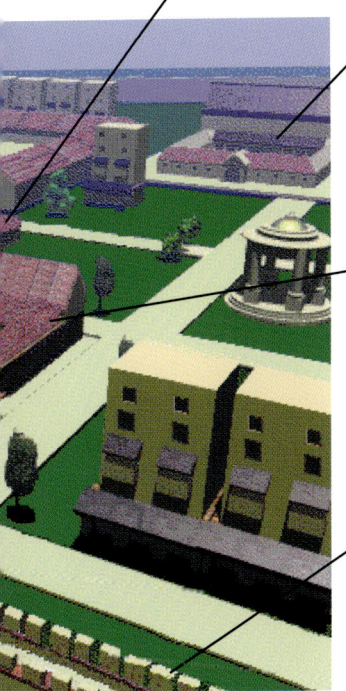

The city of Rome

At the heart of the Roman **empire** was the great city of Rome – home to more than a million people! To many people in the empire, Rome was the center of the world.

The city was full of grand public buildings, such as temples, theaters, bathhouses, and sports arenas. The streets were lined with decorated arches and statues of Rome's greatest leaders.

However, Rome also had many slum districts, where the poorer people lived in overcrowded blocks of flats, separated by narrow, dark alleys.

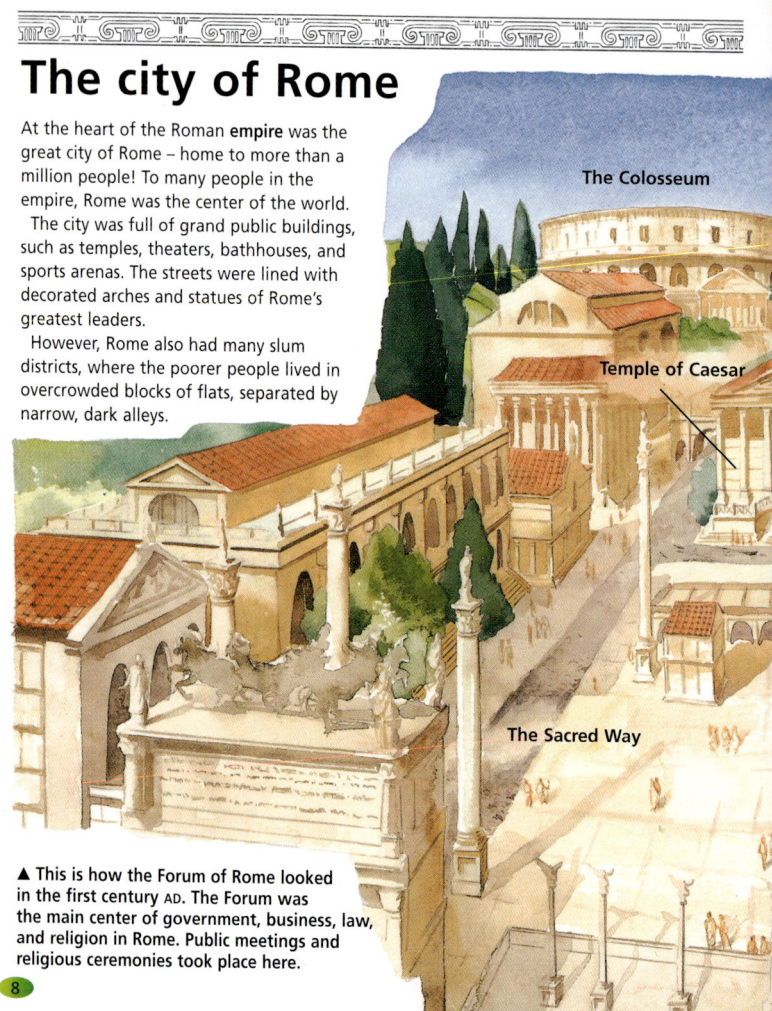

The Colosseum

Temple of Caesar

The Sacred Way

▲ This is how the Forum of Rome looked in the first century AD. The Forum was the main center of government, business, law, and religion in Rome. Public meetings and religious ceremonies took place here.

Arch of Titus

Temple of Vesta

Temple of Castor and Pollux

Basilica Julia

▲ The Forum as it looks today. Can you spot the remains of any buildings shown in the drawing?

FastFact
The first inhabitants of Rome settled there in 1000 BC.

This is how one Roman writer, called Seneca, described the great capital city:

"Look at the crowds! They come here from all over the world. Some come for entertainment, others have come to make their fortunes."

Republic and emperors

For almost 500 years, Rome was a **republic**. This meant that it was governed by a group of elected officials rather than by a single person, such as a king or an emperor. Two **Consuls** were chosen every year. They ruled with the advice of the **Senate**, a council made up of men from Rome's most important families.

The Republic broke down in a series of **civil wars**. One section of the Roman army battled against another as a group of ambitious politicians and generals fought for power.

The final victor in the civil wars was **Augustus**. In 27 BC, he made himself more powerful than the Senate and the Consuls, and became the first emperor of Rome. Emperors ruled Rome for the next 500 years. There were more than 75 emperors in all.

▼ Julius Caesar was a successful general and politician. He became ruler of Rome during the civil wars and was given the title "Dictator for Life." In 44 BC, he was killed by a group of senators who were afraid he had become too powerful.

▲ Rome's first emperor, Augustus.

Augustus (27 BC–AD 14)
Rome was peaceful and prosperous during the reign of Augustus. The Romans admired Augustus so much that after his death, the Senate declared that he had become a god!

Hadrian (AD 117–138)
The Emperor Hadrian spent years traveling all over the empire, building forts and walls, such as the one across northern Britain. Hadrian changed some of the laws of Rome to protect slaves from cruelty.

FastFact
The systems of government used in the United Kingdom and the United States today are based on the system used by the Romans.

▲ These coins show an emperor visiting London, and a new harbor at Ostia, close to Rome.

Coins
Roman coins were not just objects for buying things. Many coins had a portrait of the emperor stamped on them. This showed people throughout the **empire** what their ruler looked like. Coins were also used to announce great events, such as a military victory or a new building.

▲ The Emperor Augustus watches over the building of a new temple in Rome.

11

The Roman army

It was thanks to the army that the Romans were able to conquer and protect their huge **empire**. The Roman army was successful because it was better organized, better trained, and better disciplined than any other army of the time.

The army was divided into units of around 5,500 men called **legions**. Every legion had a number and a nickname, such as "Victorious" or "Lightning."

A Roman soldier would serve in his legion for up to twenty-five years, living in barracks or a fort with his fellow soldiers. Much of his time was spent training – practicing with weapons, or going on long marches loaded with heavy equipment.

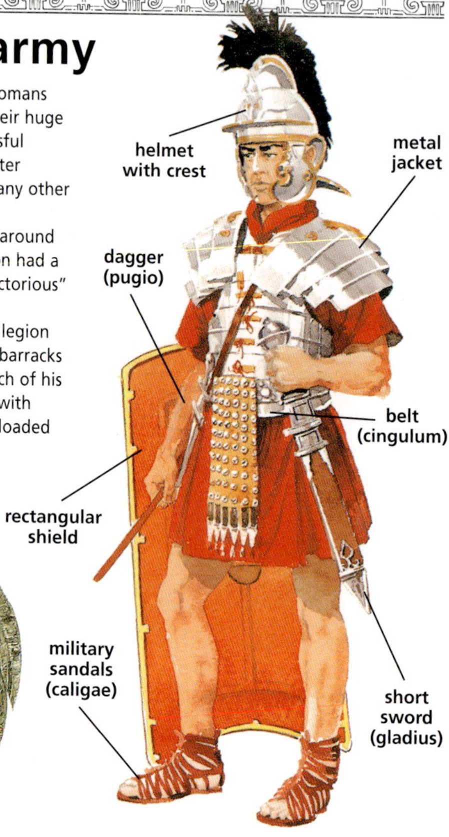

▲ An officer's decorated helmet.

▲ A legionary wore heavy armor made of overlapping plates of metal. The helmet crest was only worn for special occasions, such as victory parades.

A Roman camp

Roman army camps were usually rectangular. They were surrounded by a ditch and a wall of wooden stakes built on top of a bank of earth. Inside the camp, the soldiers pitched their tents in neat rows. When they were on the march, soldiers had to build a fresh camp each evening.

> **FastFact**
> Every legionary carried his own equipment on his long travels, including weapons, cooking pots, tools, and blankets.

Building roads

Diagram labels: drainage ditch, stone blocks, crushed stones in cement, stone slabs in cement, sand

When they were not training, fighting, or marching, the soldiers built roads. These roads were always as straight as possible, so that the army could travel quickly from one part of the empire to another. The Romans preferred to tunnel through a hill rather than take the long way around it. However, the ordinary soldiers hated road building and grumbled about it in their letters.

13

Slaves

Roman **citizens** had rights. For example, they were able to vote in elections and were given free corn to make bread. Slaves, on the other hand, had no legal rights at all.

Slaves were owned by their masters. They could be bought and sold in the market place and had to work without pay. If a slave tried to run away, he or she was often whipped or branded with a hot iron and sometimes the slaves were even killed.

Some slaves were prisoners, captured in war. Others were the children of slave parents or orphans who had been brought up by slave traders.

Slavery was an accepted part of life in Roman times. Some Romans said that slaves should be treated kindly but no one thought that slavery itself was wrong.

▼ Wealthy Romans were often carried around by their slaves in small carriages, called litters.

▲ Slaves often had to wear metal tags in case they escaped. This one says: "Hold me, lest I flee, and return me to my master Viventius."

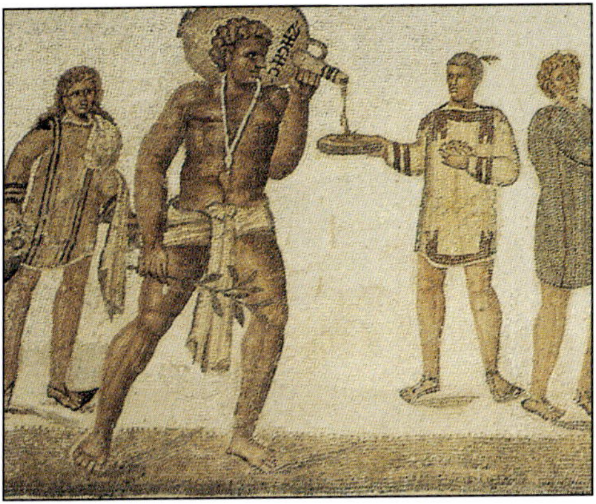

▲ An African slave pours wine for a Roman.

Gladiators

Some slaves and criminals were forced to become **gladiators** – men who fought to the death in public entertainments.

These fights were very popular. The crowds would cheer on their favorite gladiators. When the first blood was drawn, they would cry: "He's got him!" Gladiators who won many fights became as famous as film stars are today. But few lived to be old men.

Household slaves

Wealthy Romans had dozens of slaves to help them get dressed, cook for them, entertain them, and clean up after them.

Many slaves came from places outside the **empire**, such as Germany and Africa. The most highly prized slaves came from Greece and they were often better educated than their Roman masters! They served as doctors, tutors, and secretaries. Slaves who served their masters well were sometimes rewarded with their freedom.

▲ As well as fighting each other, gladiators were made to fight wild animals, such as lions and bears.

FastFact
After many wars across the world and throughout the ages, slavery is now illegal in all countries.

▲ A gladiator's dagger.

Gods and temples

The Romans worshipped many different gods and goddesses. They believed that each of the gods controlled a different part of their lives. The king of the gods was called Jupiter. His wife, Juno, was the goddess of married women and childbirth.

There were gods for almost every activity, as well as gods for places. There was even a goddess, called Cardea, who watched over door hinges!

> **FastFact**
> The Romans believed in life after death and thought that the dead went to a place called "The Underworld," which was ruled by the god Dis.

▼ Many Roman houses had shrines. Every day an offering would be left on the shrine to the gods who protected the home.

▲ This is Serapis, a Sun-god from Egypt. As the empire expanded, gods from other countries became part of Roman religion.

Christianity

The biggest change to Roman religion was the development of Christianity. The Christians believed in just one god, and they refused to worship the Roman gods. At first, the Christians were punished as criminals. But, in AD 312, the Emperor Constantine was converted to the new religion.

▶ This jug is decorated with Christian symbols.

Signs from the gods

The Romans believed that they could tell from special signs whether the gods were pleased or angry. One popular way of reading the signs was to offer food to a flock of "sacred chickens." If the chickens refused to eat the food, it was a bad sign. In the third century BC, a general called Claudius Pulcher took some sacred chickens to sea with him. He was furious when they refused to eat and threw them overboard, crying, "If you won't eat, you'll drink instead!" Soon after, he suffered a terrible defeat. People blamed it on Pulcher's treatment of the chickens.

Roman characters

Here are a few of the many characters you might see if you were able to take a trip back to the time of the Romans.

Purple trimming on the white **toga** indicated the Senator's position of power.

▶ Senator
Senators were usually men from important, wealthy families. Once elected, they served in the Senate for life. The son of a senator or wealthy citizen might also have worn a toga like this.

Laurel wreath forms a simple crown.

Purple clothes stood for wealth and power. Only the emperor was allowed to dress entirely in purple.

▶ Emperor
The emperor, also known as the First Citizen, was the most important person in the Roman Empire. He wore a white tunic with a purple toga draped over one shoulder. Togas were seen as a status symbol in Roman society. Only citizens were allowed to wear them, and slaves were forbidden from doing so.

Mercury's wand was called Caduceus. It had healing powers and Mercury used it to control people's dreams.

Mercury's lyre is similar to a harp.

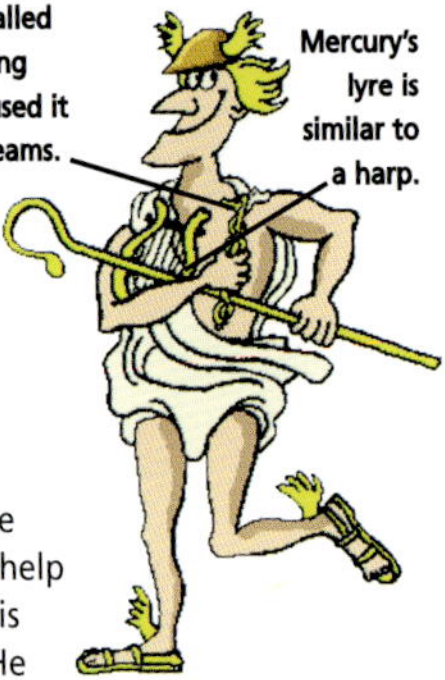

▶ Mercury
Mercury was the messenger of the Roman gods. He dashed around the heavens with the help of the wings on his hat and sandals. He also brought good luck to people and protected writers, athletes, and merchants.

Most slaves went barefoot and wore simple tunics because they were not allowed to wear togas.

▶ Slave
Slaves had few rights, little freedom and were treated like possessions by their masters. They were often bought and sold in the marketplace. Many slaves were orphans, the children of slaves, criminals, or prisoners caught during raids on other countries.

◀ **Jupiter**
- Jupiter had fiery red hair.

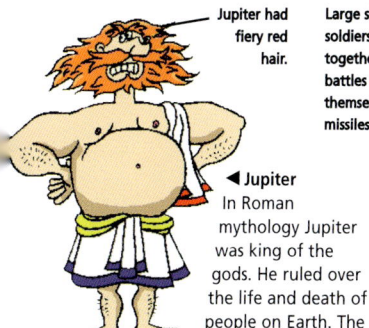

In Roman mythology Jupiter was king of the gods. He ruled over the life and death of people on Earth. The Romans believed that he could see everything and would punish bad people. Jupiter was also the god of the sky. He controlled the weather and used lightning bolts as a weapon.

◀ **Legionary**
- Large shield, which soldiers would link together during battles to protect themselves from missiles.
- Weapons, such as this dagger, swords or javelins, were always carried.

Legionaries, or foot soldiers, volunteered to join the army and were expected to serve for 25 years. They earned wages but had to pay for their own food and weapons. Legionaries carried a heavy pack of tools and provisions as they marched across vast terrritories.

▶ **Gladiator**
- Bronze helmet was worn both for protection and decoration. It often had carvings of the gods and goddesses on it.
- Metal face guard

Gladiators risked their lives in gruesome fights that were a popular form of entertainment in ancient Rome. There were many types of gladiator. Murmillos, like this one, carried a shield and wore a bronze guard on one side of the body.

▶ **Married woman**
- Roman women wore make-up, such as eye-shadow made from soot or crushed ants eggs.
- Jewelry made from gold and precious stones.

Wealthy married women could afford to wear elaborate clothes, often made of silk. Only married women could wear stolas – elegant gowns with sleeves. Women often wore their hair in braids and ringlets, or sometimes they wore a wig.

Roman baths

Every Roman town had at least one public bathhouse. Here, for a small sum, people would come each day to exercise, wash, chat, and relax.

Men and women bathed separately. The bigger bathhouses had special areas for each sex. In the smaller baths, they would bathe at different times of the day.

Each bathhouse had a courtyard for exercise, such as weightlifting, wrestling, or ball games. There was also a swimming pool and a number of rooms that were kept at different temperatures. Bathers sat and sweated in the hot room where they could also take a hot bath. Then they might move to the cold room for a quick plunge in the cold water.

cold room (frigidarium)

▼ Slaves massaged the bathers with olive oil (the Romans did not have soap) then scraped their skin clean with a curved metal tool, called a strigil.

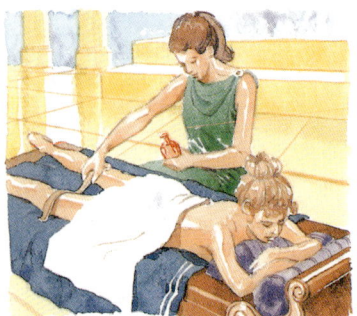

▶ Many bathers carried their own oil to the baths in jugs, such as this one.

warm room (tepidarium)

hot room (caldarium)

▼ The hot room was heated by a hypocaust system. Hot air was channeled under the floor and up through spaces in the walls.

hypocaust system

FastFact
Up to 2,000 people could bathe in the largest baths. Many of these were built in the third century AD.

▶ Roman towns needed a lot of water to supply all the bathhouses, fountains, and public pumps. Water was brought to the towns along special arched channels, called aqueducts. These carried water from nearby lakes, rivers, and springs. Many of the aqueducts ran underground, through mountains and across valleys. Some people secretly piped water into their homes so that they didn't have to pay for it!

21

Farming

Most farming was done on large estates that were owned by wealthy Romans. Each estate had a large workforce of slaves, watched over by a steward.

The most important crops were wheat, olives, and grapes. Each farm had a building where wine was made and presses that crushed olives to make oil. Many farms also had workshops for carpenters and blacksmiths, who repaired the tools and carts used on the farm.

Slaves looked after the cattle, sheep, and pigs. Oxen were used to pull the ploughs and carts that took the goods to market.

▲ Slaves harvested and threshed corn. Horses were then used to trample on it, separating the grains from the husks.

The Romans used pruning knives on their vines and olive trees.

A farmer's sacrifice

Throughout the year, Roman farmers performed religious rituals. In May, for example, a pig, a ram, and a bull would be led around the fields and then killed as a sacrifice to the god, Mars. The Romans believed that these rituals were just as important as sowing or ploughing.

How to treat your slaves

Roman landowners didn't always agree about the best way to treat their slaves. Some people thought it was better to treat slaves kindly:

"The foremen will work harder if they are rewarded. They should be given a bit of property of their own and mates from among their fellow slaves to bear them children. This will make them more steady and more attached to the farm."

But other landowners thought that slaves were no more important than the animals on the farm:

"Sell worn-out oxen, worn-out tools, old slaves, and anything else that is no longer of any use."

▼ This mosaic shows slaves gathering and treading grapes to make wine.

Food

Poor Romans lived on a very simple diet – porridge or bread made from wheat, soup made of millet or lentils, with beans, onions, turnips, olives, and pork, the cheapest meat.

In contrast, wealthy Romans could afford to buy food from all over the empire. These delicacies included pears from Syria and wine from Greece.

A Roman kitchen

Roman kitchens were usually small rooms with simple equipment. Food was fried or boiled in earthenware or bronze pots over a charcoal fire. Meat was roasted in the ashes of a small brick oven. The kitchen also had large jars of olive oil, wine, vinegar, and fish sauce, as well as a **mortar** for grinding up spices.

▼ The slaves are kept busy in the kitchen of a wealthy Roman house, preparing for a dinner party.

◀ Pottery was mass-produced for Roman kitchens. These bowls come from Sussex, in southern England.

▲ This mosaic shows a slave boy working in the kitchen.

A dinner party

Serving expensive and unusual food at a banquet was a way of showing off. Guests ate lying down on couches. They picked at the food with their fingers and often had to wash their hands during the meal.

Dinner had a number of courses. It started with an appetizer – salad, eggs, snails, or shellfish, such as sea-urchins. This was served with **mulsum**, wine sweetened with honey.

Fish and meat dishes were served as the main course. Specialities included **dormice** stuffed with pork and pine kernels, sows' udders, and roast peacock. The more unusual the food, the better! Finally, there was a sweet course of cakes and fruit.

After the meal had finished, the guests would be served more to drink while they were entertained by singers, musicians, acrobats, and story-tellers.

▲ The most popular Roman flavoring was liquamen, or fish sauce. It was made from anchovies or mackerel, which were soaked in salt water and left to rot in the Sun. It was very spicy and salty.

FastFact
Once a year, masters waited on their slaves at a banquet to celebrate Saturn, god of agriculture.

A Roman house

From the outside, the houses of wealthy Romans looked bare. They were designed to be private and safe from burglars so there were few outer windows. Instead, Roman houses faced inward, with rooms arranged around an attractive courtyard and a garden.

If you visited a Roman house, the first room you entered would be the **atrium**, a sort of entrance hall or courtyard that had an opening in the ceiling to let in light. Beneath the opening there was a basin to collect rainwater. This basin would have been the family's main water supply.

From the atrium, you would go into the **tablinum**, a sort of living room and office. This was where the head of the family would greet his daily visitors.

▲ A cut-away view of a Roman house.

Behind the tablium was the garden, which was full of flowers and ornamental statues. The most popular type of garden, called a **peristyle**, had a covered walkway around its edges, giving shade on hot summer days.

▶ The Romans decorated the walls of their homes with brightly-colored paintings. The floors were often covered in mosaic pictures made from hundreds of tiny tiles.

FastFact
In large town houses the family lived around the atrium, while the front rooms may have been rented to shopkeepers.

Make a mosaic

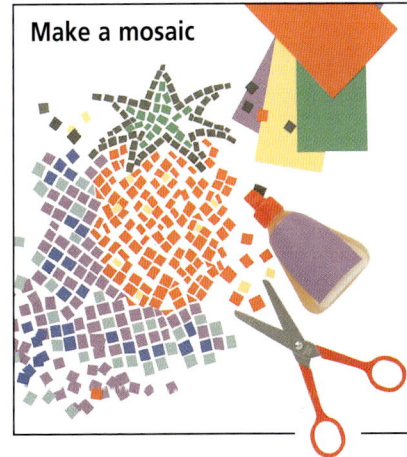

You can make a mosaic yourself at home or at school, using small squares of colored paper instead of real tiles.

● Cut several sheets of different colored paper into small squares.

● Sketch the outline of your mosaic in pencil on a sheet of plain paper.

● Then stick the colored squares in place with paper glue.

● Remember to leave a tiny space between each of your paper "tiles," so that the mosaic looks realistic.

27

Clothes

Men

Roman citizens wore a wool or linen tunic – a sort of baggy T-shirt. Over the tunic, they wrapped a toga – a big, plain, woollen sheet, arranged in a complicated system of folds. The toga was worn like a suit is today. Men wore togas in public when they wanted to look smart.

Men were usually expected to be clean shaven. This meant a painful, daily ordeal at the barbers, because the Romans did not use shaving soap. Even household slaves would be sent off to be shaved. It was a great relief for many men when the Emperor Hadrian decided to grow a beard and made shaving unfashionable.

▼ **Rich women wore beautiful jewelry set with precious stones, such as this necklace, bracelet, and brooch.**

▲ **A wealthy Roman citizen and his wife in smart dress.**

Women

Women wore a much longer tunic than men, that reached down to their ankles. Married women wore a gown with sleeves, called a **stola**, on top of their tunic.

Women's hairstyles were always changing. Hair might be piled up as high as possible, or worn in tight ringlets. Women also wore elaborate wigs. Some were jet black, made of hair imported from India. There were also blonde wigs, using hair clipped from German slave girls.

Romulus and Remus

By the time the Romans began to write down their history, Rome was already centuries old. But they told stories about their early years, to explain how their way of life had come about. This story explains how the city was founded and why it was called "Rome."

Long ago, a wicked king called Amulius ruled over the city of Alba Longa. He had stolen the throne from his elder brother, Numitor, who fled to the hills and hid among the shepherds and herdsmen.

Amulius killed Numitor's two sons and forced Numitor's daughter to become a priestess. That way, she could never marry and have children who could take power away from Amulius.

One day, Amulius was furious to hear that his niece had given birth to twin boys. She claimed that their father was Mars, the god of war, who had visited her one night in a dream. Amulius did not believe her and ordered the two boys to be drowned.

Instead of drowning the boys, Amulius' servants set them afloat on the Tiber River in a reed basket. They drifted down the river, toward the Palatine Hill, where they finally came to rest under a fig tree.

A she-wolf came across the babies, attracted by their crying. Instead of killing and eating them, she looked after the boys, feeding them with her own milk.

Soon after, an old shepherd, called

29

Faustulus, was watching his flock when he noticed the fresh tracks of a wolf. Taking his spear, he set off to find the animal to kill it. To his amazement, he found the she-wolf with the two baby boys.

Faustulus took the babies home with him and showed them to his wife, Laurentia. The old shepherd and his wife had no children of their own, although they had always longed for some. The couple decided they would bring up the boys and named them Romulus and Remus.

The twins grew up among the shepherds and herdsmen of the hills by the Tiber River. As they got older, the boys displayed such strength and cleverness that people knew they were born leaders.

One day, some herdsmen looking after the flocks belonging to Numitor accused the twins of stealing cattle. There was a fight and, in the scuffle, the herdsmen took Remus as a prisoner.

Numitor was puzzled when he met Remus. Something was strangely familiar about him. When Remus told Numitor his age and that he had a twin brother, the old man realized that he was talking to his own grandson! He was overjoyed. He told the twins who they really were, and how his wicked brother, Amulius, had wanted them dead.

Romulus and Remus agreed to help their grandfather get back the throne of Alba Longa. They led their fellow shepherds to the city and made a surprise attack on Amulius, killing him in his palace. Numitor was then welcomed back by the people of Alba Longa as the rightful king.

The twins now lived as princes in Alba Longa. But they were not happy there. They

31

missed the hills on the Tiber River, where they had grown up. Eventually, Romulus and Remus decided to go back there to found a city of their own.

Once they had reached the Tiber, the twins began to argue about where the city should be built. Remus said it should be on the Aventine Hill. Romulus said they should choose the Palatine Hill, where they had been discovered by the she-wolf.

At last, the brothers decided to ask the gods to settle the question. Each of them stood on the hill he favored and watched the sky for birds, the signs from the gods.

Soon a group of vultures began to circle, high up in the air. Six of them flew over Remus, who shouted: "Look! The gods have chosen me!"

But then twelve of the vultures flew over Romulus. Romulus began to mark out the boundary line of his city, and his followers started digging a deep trench.

Remus watched with growing anger. He began to shout insults at his brother. For a

while, Romulus ignored his brother's taunts, but when Remus and his followers started to jump over the boundary line, Romulus lost his temper. A terrible fight, using picks and shovels, broke out and Remus was killed.

Instead of showing sadness at his brother's death, Romulus just said grimly: "That's what will happen to anyone who tries to jump over my city walls!"

The new city was given the name of Rome, in honor of Romulus. He proved to be a wise king and ruled over his people for thirty-eight years.

One day, while King Romulus was watching his soldiers parade on the Field of Mars, there was a sudden thunderstorm. A thick black cloud wrapped itself around Romulus and, in a flash of lightning, he disappeared.

The Romans believed that their founding father had gone to join his father Mars up in the heavens.

How we know

Have you ever wondered how we know so much about the Romans, even though they lived so long ago?

Evidence from books

The Romans were great writers. Many of their books and letters have survived. We can still read Roman poetry, plays, and history books, as well as manuals on law, religion, warfare, farming, and cookery.

▲ This is the Arch of Titus, in Rome.

Evidence around us

The Roman way of life still influences our lives today. Many of our words come from Latin, the Roman language. Some of the names that we use for planets and months of the year come from the names of important Roman people, or figures from Roman mythology. Many of our buildings, as well as our coins, are modelled on Roman ones.

▲ Scenes on mosaics like this one tell us many things about life in Roman times.

Evidence from the ground

Archaeologists have uncovered many Roman buildings. The most spectacular discoveries are from the remains of the city of **Pompeii**. In AD 79, the volcano Vesuvius erupted and covered Pompeii in ash and mud. The remains of Pompeii were so well preserved in volcanic ash that even food cooking on a stove before the sudden eruption has been uncovered!

▲ Many people lost their lives at Pompeii. This boy was buried under the volcanic ash. When his body decayed, it left a space in the ash that archaeologists filled with plaster to make a cast.

Glossary

Abacus An instrument used by Roman school children to do their sums. It had beads that moved up and down, inside a frame.

Amphora A large pottery vessel used to transport olive oil and wine by sea.

Apollo God of the Sun in Roman mythology.

Aqueduct A type of water system, like a canal-carrying bridge, built by the Romans. It carried fresh water from lakes, rivers, and springs to their cities and towns.

Atrium The entry hall of a Roman house.

Augustus The first of the Roman emperors. He took over the Republic of Rome in 27 BC and founded the Roman empire.

Basilica A grand hall situated in each town which was the law court and bank.

Basilica Nova The last, and largest great public building built in the Forum at Rome, around AD 315.

Cinerary urn A carved marble urn in which the ashes of wealthy Romans were preserved in about AD 2.

Citizen A member of a state or nation. In Roman times, only citizens had the right to stand for election, vote, or join the legions.

Civil war A war between people belonging to the same nation.

Claudius Ruler of the Roman empire from AD 41–54. He added Britain and North Africa to the empire.

Colosseum A huge sporting arena built in Rome in AD 80. It took 10 years to build and could hold 50,000 people. The outside of the building was decorated with statues of the gods.

Consuls The two most important officials in the Roman Senate.

Diocles The best chariot racer in Rome. He retired in AD 146 after winning nearly 1,500 races.

Domus A town house belonging to a wealthy family.

Dormouse A small, furry tailed rodent similar to a mouse.

Empire A large area containing many lands and peoples, all ruled by one government. In Roman times, the rule of the emperors was also called the Empire.

Ephesus One of the richest cities in the Roman Empire. There are many ruins of this ancient city still standing in what is now Turkey.

Gladiator Men, usually slaves, criminals, or prisoners of war who were forced to fight for their lives in huge arenas, creating a bloody spectacle for the crowd who watched. They fought either each other or wild animals such as crocodiles and lions.

Hadrian's Wall A wall built across northern Britain in AD 122 by the Emperor Hadrian who ruled Rome from AD 117–138. It was 72 miles long and 13ft high and was intended to defend Roman lands from the tribes who lived in the Scottish mountains.

Hypocaust A type of central heating. Floors were held up on brick columns and hot air was channeled underneath.

Insulae Blocks of flats where most Roman people lived.

Latin The language the Romans spoke in the western part of the empire. Today, Latin forms the basis of many modern European languages such as Italian, French, and Spanish.

Legion A division of the Roman Army, made up of around 5,500 men.

Liquamen A sauce made from rotten fish.

Monarchy A monarchy is ruled by a king or queen. Usually, when a king or queen dies, their son or daughter becomes the next ruler. Rome was ruled by a monarchy for more than 250 years.

Mortar A stone bowl that was used to grind spices.

Mosaic A picture made from tiny tiles.

Mulsum Wine sweetened with honey.

Pantheon A huge Roman temple built in the city of Rome to honor all the gods.

Peristyle The garden of a Roman house with a covered walkway around its edges.

Pompeii Roman city buried and preserved below volcanic ash during the eruption of Mount Vesuvius in southern Italy in AD 79.

Praetorian Guard The name given to the emperor's bodyguards.

Republic A state ruled by elected officials instead of by a king or an emperor.

Senate The Roman governing council, which was made up of men from the most important families. The council gave advice to the Consuls and, later, to the emperor.

Stola A gown with sleeves, worn by married women on top of a long tunic.

Strigil A metal tool for scraping dirt and oil off the skin.

Stylus A pointed instrument used by Roman school children to scratch letters and words into wax tablets.

Tablinium The records office situated in each town.

Tablinum The most important room in a Roman house, which served as a reception room and office.

The Laws of the Twelve Tables A special document, written in 450 BC, laying down the laws governing Rome. It outlined the way that property was bought and sold, how contracts should be agreed upon, and how criminals should be punished.

Toga A plain, rectangular piece of material worn by Roman men, which they wrapped around their bodies.

Triumphal arch Many of these were built throughout the Roman Empire, sometimes to commemorate particular achievements. They were decorated with columns, carvings, and statues of gilded bronze.

Venus Goddess of love in Roman mythology.

Activity Space
Photocopy this sheet and use it to make your own notes.

Activity Space
Photocopy this sheet and use it to make your own notes.

Draw your own Roman city

43

Questions and answers

Maximus and Claudius are the two most important men in the Roman Senate. They are the two **Consuls**. Consuls are elected every year. The Senate was the Roman governing council, made up of men from the most important families. These men were very wise and noble so Maximus and Claudius can answer all of your questions about the ancient Roman civilization.

Did Roman children go to school?
Most children didn't go to school, instead they worked in the family farm or business. Children of slaves usually became slaves themselves. Only wealthy people could afford to send their children to school, which was divided into two types. The first type was for boys and girls, aged 7–11 years. They learned reading, writing, and arithmetic. They were also taught to speak and write in **Latin** and sometimes Greek. After this, girls stayed at home to learn the skills they would need when they got married. Boys usually continued at school to learn poetry, history, and philosophy.

Maximus

What language did the Romans use?
The Romans spoke and wrote in a language called Latin. As soldiers and merchants traveled, they helped to spread Latin around the **empire**. Latin was used as long ago as 600 BC and today it still forms the basis of many modern European languages. such as English, Italian, French, and Spanish.

How did the Romans count?
Until about 500 years ago, most people in Europe used the Roman system of counting. Seven symbols called Roman numerals were used to do sums. Each symbol stood for a number: I=1; V=5; X=10; L=50; C=100; D=500; M=1,000. Two was written as II, but rather than writing IIII for four, it was written as one before five, or IV, while six was one after five, or VI. Nine is another funny one like four, and rather than being VIIII, it became one before ten, or IX. Other examples are 24=XXIV and 47=XLVII.

What were the Roman religious beliefs?
The Romans believed in many gods and goddesses. They built temples in which they worshiped and prayed to them and asked for favors. Ceremonies took place in which offerings and sacrifices were made to keep the gods happy. Emperor Augustus and all the emperors after him were worshiped as gods as they had been such great leaders. But by about AD 64, religion began to change. A new set of beliefs, called Christianity, began to develop. The Romans punished the Christians for not

worshipping the emperor, but eventually, Christianity became the dominant religion around the world and has continued to exist for nearly 2,000 years.

What were the names of some of the Roman goddesses and gods?

There were many Roman goddesses and gods. They were believed to have magical powers and to rule over different areas of life. Jupiter was king of the gods. He was married to his sister Juno, the ruler of women and childbirth. Vulcan was god of fire, Diana was goddess of the Moon, **Venus** was goddess of love, **Apollo** was god of the Sun, Neptune was god of water, and Vesta was goddess of the home and the kitchen fire. Messages were conveyed between the gods by Mercury.

Have any parts of the Roman civilization survived?

Many Roman buildings still stand today, such as the **Colosseum** in Rome and **Hadrian's Wall** along the border between England and Scotland in the United Kingdom. The Romans influenced modern life in other ways as well. Roman literature and works of art are still read and seen today and have influenced artists throughout the ages. Some months of the year are named after Roman gods and leaders, for example August is named after the Emperor Augustus and March is named after the god Mars. Likewise, the planets Mercury, Venus, Jupiter, and Mars are named after Roman gods.

How did the Romans entertain themselves?

Throughout the year there were many holidays and festivals, most based on religious beliefs. Gods and goddesses were celebrated on certain days. Public entertainment included gladiator battles, animal fights, and chariot races. On a more relaxing note, there was music, theater, and the baths, where people played games and exercised, in addition to washing. The wealthy frequently held grand dinner parties.

Claudius

How did the Romans travel?

In cities, people tended to walk. With so many people on the streets, chariots and carts with wheels were banned. The very wealthy were carried around in a litter – a small carriage, carried by slaves. Chariots were used for races, parades, and processions, while horse-drawn coaches carried people and goods outside the cities. Mail was generally delivered on horseback. The Romans built around 50,000 miles of roads that criss-crossed the empire. Many of the roads were built by the army as they moved into new territories. Ships carried goods around the Mediterranean and from the seas beyond the empire.

Index

A
aqueducts 6, 21
army 10, 12–13
atrium 26

C
Caesar, Julius 10
Christianity 16, 45
citizens 14
civil wars 10
clothes 5, 19, 28
coins 11, 34
Colosseum 8, 45
Consuls 10, 44
cooking 24, 34
criminals 15, 16
crops 22

E
emperors 10, 11, 16, 18, 28
empire 5, 6, 8, 12, 13, 15, 24, 44
  see also 'Roman Empire'

F
farming 22–23, 34
food 24–25

Forum 7, 8, 9

G
gladiators 15, 19, 45
goddesses 16, 44, 45
  Cardea 16
  Juno 16
gods 5, 11, 16–17
  Jupiter 16, 19
  Mars 29, 33
Greece 15, 24

H
houses 7, 8, 21, 26–27
hypocaust 21

J
jewellery 19, 28

L
Latin 5, 34, 44
liquamen 25
litters 14, 45
legionary 12, 13, 19
legions 12

M

mortar 24
mosaics 23, 25, 27
mulsum 25

P

peristyle 26–27
Pompeii 34
public baths 7, 8, 20–21, 45

R

religion 8, 16, 34, 44, 45
Republic 10

roads 5, 13, 45
Roman Empire 5, 11
Rome, city of 8–9, 10, 29, 33
Romulus and Remus 29–33

S

sacrifices 23, 44
Senate 10, 18
shrines 16
slaves 11, 14, 15, 18, 20, 22, 23, 25, 28
soldiers 12, 13, 19
stolas 19, 28

strigils 20

T
tablinum 26, 27
temples 6, 8, 9, 11, 44
togas 18, 28

V
Vesuvius 34

W
wigs 19, 28
wine 15, 22, 23, 25

Published by
Two-Can Publishing LLC
234 Nassau Street
Princeton, NJ 08542

www.two-canpublishing.com

Copyright © 2001, Two-Can Publishing

For information on Two-Can books and multimedia, call 1-609-921-6700, fax 1-609-921-3349, or visit our Web site.

All rights reserved. No part of this publication may be reproduced, stored in a retrieval system or transmitted in any form or by any means electronic, mechanical, photocopying, recording or otherwise, without prior written permission of the publisher.

Author: Peter Crisp
Consultant: Emma Dench

"Two-Can" is a trademark of Two-Can Publishing
Two-Can Publishing is a division of
Zenith Entertainment Ltd,
43–45 Dorset Street, London W1H 4AB

Hardback ISBN 1–58728–753–6
Hardback 1 2 3 4 5 6 7 8 9 10 02 01 00

Photograph Credits:
Ancient Art and Architecture Collection:
front cover, p.11 (top right), p.12, p.23 (top left), p.24;
Bridgeman Art Library: p.16 (bottom right),
p.25 (bottom right), p.27, p.37 (bottom right);
Bruce Coleman: p.21, p.34 (bottom right), p.35;
CM Dixon: p.15, p.16 (top right), p.25 (top left);
ET Archive: p.11; Michael Holford: p.14, p.20,
p.23 (bottom), p.28, p.34 (left), p.34 (top right),
p.36, p.47; Zefa: p.9

Illustrations on pages 29–33 are by Maxine Hamil.
Illustrations on pages 6–7, 18–19 and 44–45 are by
Jeffrey Lewis, Carlo Tartaglia, Jon Stuart and Alan Rowe.
All other illustrations are by Gillian Hunt.

Reproduced by Next Century, Hong Kong
Printed by Wing King Tong, Hong Kong

This title previously published in a large format.